Also by Thomas Rabbitt   *Exile* (1975)

The Booth Interstate

ALFRED A. KNOPF   NEW YORK   1981

THOMAS RABBITT
The Booth Interstate

Some of the poems included here have appeared in other
publications: *Esquire*, *Poem*, and *Shenandoah*.

Library of Congress Cataloging in Publication Data
Rabbitt, Thomas [date]
The Booth interstate
(Knopf poetry series; 4)
I. Title. II. Series.
PS3568.A22B6   1981   811'.54   80-7975
ISBN 0-394-51382-7
ISBN 0-394-73962-0 (pbk.)

Manufactured in the United States of America
First Edition

For My Mother

Contents

Part One

Part Two

The Booth Interstate

Part One

Gargoyle

He looks down to watch the river twist
Like a dead vein into the suburbs.
From his height it is all flat, stone-grey
And ugly. He knows he himself is hideous,
Sterile, the artist's pleasantry set up
To scare off devils. He knows nothing.
He is stunning in his pure impossibility.
Enough cherry trees blossom along the river.
Enough paired lovers gaze through the pink air.
Drab birds, disguised as money, sing prettily
And the sun blinds itself in the water.
He hears laughter. He knows nothing.
When the lovers glance up, they take him in.
Their looks are incidental, monumental, sweeping.

The Old Sipsey Valley Road

Booths knew nothing either. They built themselves in.
They owned pines, tin houses, some collapsing barns.
They *owned* them. Fields, gullies taking the fields,
And a pocked blacktop curving out of sight
Downhill into Coker and a brown lake
And the brick houses that needed to make
Head or tail of the face hidden in the hill.
The first Booth fell out of the sky one day,
Without a mule or pickup, nothing his,
Belonging to a fear who had devised him,
Who had sent him to the hill to claim
He could clear the brush from the fields for free
If he could have the wood. Someone said, Yes,
And that was it and then the scrub pine closed in.

Doodle Hill

1

After sixty years it still is best not to think
Of him lifting away from her legs like lard.
He is dead—husband, lover—and death is hard
And the chair is hard and *my sons' goats stink!*
The porch swings under her chair. Her violets stink
Like a wreath on the rail. Boothtown's hard
On incest, hard on boys and pigyards and the girls
Who see their brothers returning from the fields
With quail and smiles and fall down in the cowshed
After supper's laid and done. *Chester dead?*
Chester dear, who never was worth baconfat in bed,
Is dead and my violets breathe like idiots
I've named my—our—children for. Idiots.
The goats increaseth and should all be killed.

2

Her sons masturbate in the woods behind the house.
She used to watch wondering was she right or proud.
The gullies smelled of kudzu — grape lollipops —
And the boys posed in an awkward crowd
Of arms and legs, like cyclones come to ruin
The haybales stacked up in the shapes of barns.
They're rotting the land. Steadily. Like rain.
Nothing can be gathered for the wet destroys.
Her boys went free. Next day was always dark.
She would watch at dawn from the front of the house
While like a yellow slug the school bus came
And with its air brakes harvested her boys.
Each morning she is too pale, old and stark
To be gathered in or saved by such strange young arms.

Boy with a Knife

Six a.m. The boy at your bathroom sink
Has offered you a shave. By then, you're dead.
By eight you've breakfasted. He's given you
His name. You recognize the obscene wink,
The hand on your thigh, blades come to a head.
You see cows hungry at the fence, a view
Of the road to town lined by boys with knives,
Each granted a bed in the back of your truck.
Supper comes. You've cut off like wives
The balls of a dozen pigs. One day's wreck.
Stricken, chilled, you eat what you've hurt
And make yourself ready for bed. His knife
Owns the sheet between you like a common heart.
You know: this is all you have made of your life.

The Runner

The runner counts. Each step he takes he counts.
Again. Again. His heart opens and closes
Like a rose. He is chasing someone's horses
Down the dusty road, chasing his body
Backwards through dust. It's time he counts:
His lungs, his steps; along the fence, the roses
Dropped on barbs like blood; and he counts the horses,
Their hooves, their steps as they surround a boy
At the end of the road, divide and then
Refuse themselves in clouds of dust they've raised
And into which they disappear like ghosts.
The runner's counting might postpone the end
Or he might recognize the boy: he's earned
This kiss, the self he counts among his lusts.

The Weatherman

Dell Booth found out that TV was the key
To the future. The news brought hope: a frost
In Florida meant that oranges cost
Much more. So the Booths spent every night
Deciphering a new agronomy:
To eat a slice of the moon was one way
Of growing rich, and when the signs were right
The Booths descended on the A&P
To buy up all the frost-bit tangerines.
Next spring Boothtown lied: *Boothtown's planting beans.*
All summer long young Booths in pickup trucks
Straddled girlfriends who claimed that they could see
The citrus grow between their limbs. They see
In the hogbriar only their own green wrecks.

Duchess Booth

I

For fifty-seven years her hair is red
And her bright pinafores amaze the flowers.
I find her mornings rummaging the garbage
In my barrels or picking up the feathers
Near the coop. Her name is Mary Alice Booth,
But you may call me Duchess. One child said:
Duchess Booth is fixing to make you dead.
We sometimes speak. The beer cans are for salvage,
The feathers for her wings because, with grace,
She plans to die a virgin, the one Booth
Who enters into heaven while the others
Cry mercy at the gate. There is a place
For her there, among the ancient thrones and powers.
Before she spoke I thought love might be dead.

2

His sweater smelled of perfume. It wasn't his.
Duchess's maybe, or some girl he'd put on
And off too often. Sometimes before
The smell of some girl would stay in the wool
Like beer or the word he wouldn't stop giving
Till she had it. He stood outside somewhere,
Put one arm into the other. The kiss
He found was himself—wrapped up, done in,
Tied down by what he'd said. So he was singing
In the parking lot outside a bar. Why
Whisper? *Old Duchess wanted her a fool.*
No woman's worth the time it takes to piss!
He tried to think of girls who didn't cry.
Without love he could stay to drink some more.

3

She saves Christmas paper for the fire barrel.
Later she finds bows, spangles, small parts
Of a life reversing itself like film.
She feeds a lost lover into the barrel.
Children emerge, a flowered dress, the hearts
Of hens still beating in her squeezing palm.
Memories make me sleep or else I'll cry.
She wrings its neck. *The hen won't ask me why
The sun comes up, why chickens be.* She knows
Exactly where on the highway one year
One lover died. His skull split in her hands.
She tries to understand all the dark roads.
They lead inside. She says she loves him more
Each time she tries to burn him off her hands.

4

Before the drive back to Boothtown they sat
In his truck while the Deadwood Grill sign flashed
Warnings through her. She cried. She said she'd curse
His harlots and he'd give them up because
She wouldn't leave enough alive to hold.
She would see it soon, she said—his skull spill
In moonlight and his brains swim out like fish.
She knew: she was too old for him, too fat,
And she'd said his hands on her breasts were cold.
The road home sprouted trees. His pickup crashed
Clearing pine in its rush down Lindsay Hill.
She woke alone and climbed back to the road.
Her hands could not contain his spilling pulse,
And his kept rummaging her neon dress.

The Abandoned Brickyard

What's left of their hope is a stack that rises
Through rubble like the periscope the dead
Thrust up to see the girl inside. She'll wake
To watch the disk of sky darken in crisis,
The boys gone with her clothes, her gooseflesh red
With semen, sweat and brickdust. She will take
Her time getting up and she will not cry
Until she thinks she hears the boys return.
She stares up the blind funnel into night
Where fires roll like billiards on the black sky.
She feels rough hair brush her legs and breath burn
Her breasts, and she thinks she will die of fright.
The tongues foraging her flesh say her name.
Their word is *whore*, for the dead know her shame.

A Still Life

They go down, the lively, deadly colt to graze
And his dam who must follow him through the heat
To the pond. The fields fall and rise under a haze
And the hills and trees half make as in a print.
This is old. Surrounded by drought. A horseman stands
Unhorsed in the left corner by a rock, near a tree.
The horseman sees the least. He holds his hands
To his eyes, frames fingers to hold what he can see.
Not far from him both horses are grazing
Beside the dark water. Both are almost still.
What moves is a light breeze playing
Their manes and tails forward. All face the last hill.
Over it the evening is rising. The horseman has turned
Too late. He cannot face what he has learned.

Briar Rose

1

The widow Belle clearing briars from her yard
Imagines she is chasing off the snakes
Like preachers drive out sin. In January
Death lies down and grafts itself to roots.
In thorns grown thick what stands is as hard
As the ground where she finds the boy asleep.
She runs inside and forgets. In February
All women think of spring and soon new shoots
Will sprout and all the winter's work unmade.
One buys a blade. In March she thinks that goats
Can keep the briars down. She forgets the blade,
The goats, she forgets the month. It's still cold.
She sets fire to the hollow where she found
Her son; she watches while the color eats the ground.

2

For three days he's lain hidden in the woods
Above her house. He's been dreaming her,
Waiting hard for some sign of her distress.
At sunset he crawls down through mud and weeds
To listen at her door. He hears nothing new:
Crates scrape, dragged across the floor; her dress
Ripped on a trunk lock. There is cold air rushing
With her room to room. He crawls up the hill.
Late morning, the last time, she's out to feed
The dogs and chickens, fur and feathers brushing
Her pale blotched legs. He thinks the dogs must feel
Her fine touch, almost want to make her bleed.
He wants to ask her why she has to leave.
In the thorns he confuses his dream with rage.

Pastoral

John Junior in a white pickup is leading
An unbroke grey mule over Lindsay Hill.
The dust of their passage reddens the air.
Booth dogs cry havoc and the mule keeps trying
To climb the pickup's bumper. You can't kill
Young mules, John says. The right foreleg is bleeding.
The dogs go crazy, smelling blood and fear.
And nearby, gravely, Duchess Booth is crying.
John stops the truck and gets out with his whip
Snaking behind him in the dust. One crack
Is all it takes to get the nearest dog,
Its leg wrapped round and snapped. The others slip
Into the ditch. You need, he says, to break
Young stock to lead or else your ass'll drag.

Poe's Last Stand

It's 1849 and I should vote
Many times, or the coma will not come.
It's my last campaign for democracy,
The sweet hurrah she's played for France and me.
Mister Key! Mister Key, I think your tune
Is awful. Oh say, can who see, they shout.
The rockets glare like angry lunatics
While night and wild horses come down on us.
Illuminations will not do! My vote
Comes in a brown pint like word from shipwrecks,
Here to Fort McHenry, the corpses' choice,
Drownings most of us, for the Whigs won't float.
I'll have my drink and register my *X*.
The dead man's stroke must *seem* anonymous.

The Swimmers *(for Robert Lowell)*

The girl swims backwards from the shore.
Her eyes fill with towers and the sad light
Falling like the sun to earth. This is more
Than she has earned, more than she deserves, she might
Still say if she could speak. She thinks she'll drown.
The boy swims dangerously underneath
The girl. He reaches up to pull her down
To a new lover. Now, for one breath,
Their lungs explode, their limbs are baffled
By the closing pressures of the sea's heart.
What drives him is crawling from the sludge
Back to the sea. What in her is awful
He saw also in himself. Her broken heart
Drives down and darkly to the vegetating edge.

The Cape Drownings

1 *Falmouth Heights*

You thought you swam from here through marriage,
A death's-head sidestroke through Vineyard Sound.
You had courage, following the procession of devils
The tide in your womb could die of.
We had two beds, neither ours, but did our best.
You are a good ghost, the kind who
Ages leather and keeps the insides soft, comfortable.
I saw you, an old lady, cross on will to West Chop,
Walking from the jetty near the Oak Crest Inn.
Around a sick heart, like a grandmother, you wore
Rubber wading slippers and your love of spectacle.
You saw yourself at eighty coming out of the sea
With your hair streaming and a bouquet of razors
And a deed to each bed in the hotel.

2   *Pride's Crossing*

I remember a cow straddling the tracks
Like your mother in her Boylston Street dress
The day of the wedding. The great homes ride uphill
As they must, and the Cape Ann local eats each tie
To the Crossing. I remember the Cherry Hill Dairy,
Baptisms postponed for the *News*, the prize
Of your death from Gloucester. You walked to the fleet
Through the muddy smell of Gorton's and the fish girls.
Up to their pits in oysters, you said.
What do they know of motif or money, the fine art
Of lobster? If the fleet could sail to the Crossing!
Do you remember when the cows broke loose and drowned
Between the ties? when the rich mothers ran down
With buckets because of a rumor of pearls?

Casino Beach

At night the sand wears a corsage of flesh.
She can smell it. The boy is hard, strange,
A summer storm moving in to plague her
With the things he's done. Over the Heights
The wind brings fog. Wind and fog derange
Her new life. Under them, the phosphors flash
And she cries because the season's almost over.
She has waited all her life for these nights.
The boy's thin face disappears. He has tried.
He cannot take her in before she dies.
She tells him she has built a wall
Around herself, an illness, what the papers call
Cancer. She is a fist, a thing everyone pries
Open finger after finger for the small change inside.

Views from the Bridge

1 *Crane*

I could recreate today on the bridge:
The Captain watches for eagles at sea
And his mates are scared of my rattlesnake.
Should I still be reaching back for the ring?
I simply do not know. This near the edge
What I see is Mexico and an old girl
Who thinks she's given me the chance I'll take
To be a man. She's buried me
In romance, enough reality to hurl
Me over. No lifeline there. There's a boy
Who doesn't want to read about the church
I found too beautiful to leave alone.
I had to write its bells. Let them all search.
I'll sink into my own words like a stone.

2 Berryman

Forever I have complicated lies,
Though my testicles seem to stay in place.
I've drunk my way down, up here: fire and ice,
Black tongues, pussy cats and booze. And the glass
That launched my final slip. I could let go
But for the strange man hanging to my neck
Who's still afraid. I look up at the snow
Or I could, falling, look up from the book
I'd write at home were I not already dead
Nearly, though unlaunched, hung at the edge
Of a genius I cannot force myself to shake.
Black heart, let me show you some lies I've said
And you can show me yours. And let love take
Us back from there. Mistakes have been our bridge.

The Weight Room

The weight room tiled with mirrors is no place
To want to be alone. The modesty
You claim is just another of your lies.
Cosmetic is the word you use for lifting
As if the weights gave strength to lift your face
Out of the grave. The mirror's surgery
Reverses everything except the eyes.
Bodybuilding might be one way of shifting
Your body's guilt back into your own hands.
You might believe the young man opposite
Is you, pumping up with curls—but he smiles,
A thing you could not do. Just where he stands
Is where you want to be—if you could fit
And not bloody your body or the tiles.

At the Movies

A lion roars and the theater seethes with blond men
And women. The wicked, you think, are safe
Among the blond, but then
The hero comes on, tall, blue-eyed, wealthy
And proud, and you believe the hero knows:
You are the image he hates in himself.
You shout for a plot: Camera! and on it rolls
To show the hero and his girl under a leafy heaventree
And all the audience watching in the shadows.
You think, No, in the movies it shouldn't ever be
Like this. This grim seduction on a park
Bench is not what you paid to see.
You shout again: Curtain! Lights! and in the strict
Glare you find lovers killing and eating the dark.

Part Two

The Märchen *(for Randall Jarrell)*

I

Then, Hansel, even your sister was older
And wiser than you. The witch had stripped you
Past your underwear and you had to stand
Naked until she'd got it right in stone.
You still feel the sculptor's hand on your shoulder,
Her breath modeling your neck. Your own hand
Runs for cover. Now that you're nearly grown
And can call yourself *survivor*, do you
Regret your fear? All mothers should be made
To suffer passions for their handsome sons.
No war is cruel enough, no death too young.
The stuffed animals all died. The witch paid
For her fantasies. There were other sons.
Your mother did not miss you very long.

2

The trouble is, Hansel, you really are
The girl next door, the fileclerk at the zoo,
The housewife eyeing bagboys at the store.
You're all things to everyone but you.
If you stand on the highway long enough
The traffic will succeed where you have failed.
You will be changed, though your change is the stuff
Failure's made of. The fileclerk will have failed.
The bus that's like a bus runs down a tiger
Like a tiger as if it were a cat.
The housewife chooses boys instead of soap.
The vulture when he comes will have no answer
Because you've changed and let your question lapse.
You might be saved, if all it took was hope.

Rape

The men chase the boy into the hog shed.
When the pigs panic and the walls collapse,
He runs to the house, to his mother's bed
Where one man finds him underneath. He laughs.
The boy scurries deeper into the dust.
More men arrive. He doesn't understand.
An unrolled condom strikes out like a snake.
A pink fur slipper fills the air with must.
The man's laughter sounds outdoors, like the wind
Over the storm cellar. He smells the smoke
But will not move until his mother comes.
She never does. While the dust ruffle glows
Like a flaming sun on four horizons,
The men turn away and the boy's death grows.

Lot Booth's Wife

The glaze her eyes break through is grief
For boys she left in town, the pretty one
Who one night touched her breast. Her daughters stare.
Perhaps they really hope death will relieve
The family. The hard eye of the sun
Is eating Boothtown's best parts. The red air
Raises the noise and stench toward God.
Only this fire can clear her name.
On the innocent sky the angels write with light:
Booth's wife no longer cares for Booth or God.
Her daughters have their city boys to shame.
Booth's wife has her sons and their hands at night
When she goes to the loft and the walls fall
And she dreams more than truth or salt can tell.

Survivors

One or two manage to crawl from the pit
At Babi Yar. One goes to America.
One, mortally hurt, is hiding in a half-burned barn.
Nearby, a chameleon changes from wall to door
To charred as it scuds toward heat.
One thinks: This is the end of the world.
One disagrees: In America you are so nearly free . . .
If you move any closer it will spit
In your eye. One *must* disagree.
From out of the blue, megaphones translate
One kind of order into noise: Don't be dead
Longer than you must. One and another turn,
As in a dream, trapped between color and flight,
Change and fear, into one another. One is made free.

Mother Russia's Twins

1   *Yesenin*

I suspect the poplars drop a fine blond ash
This year. The Russian woods are dry,
Or drought is rumor and rain is everywhere
But here. Or there is fire everywhere
And for all we in Moscow know the world's a lie,
And all we're told is trash.
The state is trash.
My old dog is dead. *He cannot die.*
Three wives, a revolution and our fear,
The spite in my people's crazy eyes, the crash
Of sudden times will not dry up and burn and die.
Leave me, please, and wooden Russia as we were.
I am thirty and I wish to die.
Farewell my friend in blood, this fine red ash.

2 *Mayakovski*

My scorn for what is wood and old was art
And you were past. I loathed your lilac blood,
Your hangman's end. The mechanical bear
Was Russia then and then was everywhere.
Steel forged for me the only good.
Glass grew, bolts bloomed, the Brooklyn Bridge was art!
Somehow I have become the trousered cloud
I thought was just a dream. *I caught your fear.*
I've missed the poplars and the dance, my part
In song. Russia's requiem becomes a cloud.
You were all correct: one must care
To be beautiful. Steel, my old grey god,
Hours like these, is a gun aimed at my heart
And, as they say, the incident is closed.

Coon Hunt

Dell's hounds leap like the damned around the trunk
Of a water oak, biggest in my swamp.
Our flashlights flood the stage, the coon our star
Dimmed by the floating shadows of the leaves.
Later we move to dry ground to get drunk.
Home is close; still we call the hillside camp.
We build a fire, stare through the light it weaves
And make up lies about the Asian war
We fought. Dell struggles to take off his boot.
There's a puckered stump where his toes should go.
He calls up Tay Ninh and a jungle mine
Cong soldiers set for him. Truth is, he shot
Himself one night at home. I say I know
Chinese, that I have shrapnel in my spine.

Weathercock

Upholding the top of the barn should leave
Him time to think about a wife and son,
Their house, their plans. Instead he thinks of love.
Each year the river floods, recedes. The hot sun
Bathes the stones, the Holsteins strolling past.
His brass eyes suffer sunlight badly. The winds strive
Against him. Afire at night the dry stones rattle
In the riverbed: love. He prays strong light
Reflected off the water will drive the cattle
Over the embankment: love. He knows the moon was cast
Of bronze and set adrift in clouds sour with rain.
He knows the earth turns at his feet, day and night,
The sky turns above him. He knows things cleave
To him, the wind, the light, to prove themselves alive.

Pig Kill

1

The old sow struggles in the cattle chute.
A dozen men and boys stand by with prods
To move her to the gate. Her wicked eyes
Like slits into another world accuse
Us all of torture. It should take one shot.
She squeals each time we stick her with our goads.
Dell lifts his rifle, aims between her eyes,
Fires twice. She looks as if she will refuse
To die and shakes her head. Dell shoots to kill.
She has looked away and is staring up
The barn's tin wall toward open sky. Dell shouts
At me to grab her ear and hold her still.
I do and shield my eyes. We cannot stop
To save her now, not after fifteen shots.

2

Dell Booth knows all the universal lies:
The one about his daddy scalding hogs
With all of Boothtown gathered at the farm;
How beneath a scaffold a great pot boils
And the sow hangs in clouds of steam and flies.
The women cook. The children tease the dogs
With scraps. Dell's stories have a special form
That, all truth aside, nothing in them spoils
The lie. He can't say how he could have climbed
The scalding pot, why no one noticed him
Until too late. They turned to hear him scream.
Events, Dell says, that come from God are timed
Just right. Dell hadn't even learned to swim
Before his daddy pulled him from the steam.

3

Dell Booth would never think in terms of waste,
And yet he has a recipe for souse
Containing parts that have no other use
Now that the pig is dead. Meat from the head
And sometimes the feet is boiled, chopped fine, laced
With vinegar and pressed under a plate.
Here is a lesson for the overweight,
The pickled, those otherwise in dread
Of the blind marksman coming from the house
To the barn: with thought, nothing goes to waste.
He wears the sow's skull atop his own head.
Dell Booth is drunk, he says, as though it's news
To me. Headcheese is an acquired taste.
Whatever we eat, we're eating what's dead.

Painting My House with Blood

It takes so much it hurts and yet
She dies easily, my enemy, fit
Between the hammer and my thumb.
If you kiss your elbow, your sex will change;
This much takes work. Her lips are numb.
Who'd have thought one's bones could range
So far? that one young wife had so much blood
In her? Six quarts. As much as anyone.
Murderous, the urge to go from numb to blood.
The house clots under the sun.
Monster. Enemy. Flesh that will not quit.
The clapboards run. The task upsets the man
In me from gable down to grave and yet
We cannot stop until the colors fit.

The Dancing Sunshine Lounge

The calendar is ironic. The stripper dances
On my table, her toes awash in beer.
Ash Wednesday drags in once a year. This year
Thursday brings a dust storm from the west.
The day is airborne Oklahoma, a breast
That Lent would like to bare against the east.
The sun comes closer. A silver cast —
Her shield, this target — tarnishes the air.
The stripper's memorial body chances
My hands, my broken glass. She can't care.
We are washing down traildust, we rich dead
Who have blown in, frantic, on the wind,
And she thinks we must be paralyzed with fear.
She can't care. She loves us each like a friend.

Sappho

The hinged fangs fold back in her closing mouth
Like old words, rescinded. Noise in the coop
Is about her: old lies, cows milked, a barrel hoop
She makes when she takes her tail in her mouth.
Hoop. Whip. Race. Rat. Milk. Old words like old lovers
Have turned against her and the rooster crows
Alarm. Alarm? What hurt she knows she knows
To pit against herself. Heat. Cold. Old lovers
Deserve the cool flagstones and the sun's heat
Beating down somewhere near the sea's hard edge.
Above her the axblade glints and poses
And then comes down, and again comes down to defeat
The slow length, the coil, the color, the bright surge
Of her song severed into so many moving losses.

County Roads *(for Richard Hugo)*

1

You search out Bull Slough Road to slake your thirst
For evidence of how things get a name.
You find instead the preservation plaque:
John Byler built a road not far from here
In 1822, Alabama's first.
First is something, reason enough for fame.
When you find John Byler's road you'll go back,
Northport to the Tennessee, where somewhere
You will have to pay a toll. Settlers did.
When Union soldiers came the road was free
And now so free it isn't even here.
You'd turn for home except your truck has slid
Into the mud and stopped against a tree.
If the cows could, they'd tell you that you're there.

2

No one drives Bone Camp Road expecting more
Of life, especially yours — one more marker
To tell you why you've turned this far from home
On so remote a road. The Bone Camp Church
Is Methodist, the graveyard full, but poor.
Since 1853 nobody's home
Who counts, except perhaps the Beards. You search
The stones for clues. The afternoon grows darker
Than it should and the road you followed in
Is running out without you. Pavement rots
Under your wheels. The Choctaw camp shows through
The asphalt: this way to an extinction.
One reason for the ribs that look like ruts
Can't be traffic. There's no one here but you.

In a Dry Well

He dreamed that hungry weevils crawled
Into the cotton flower of the women, but
At daybreak the hangman came to the shaft
To say, The women are safe.
Our fine women are always safe.
What am I, he asked, to be left dangling
At the bottom of a dry well? No one answered.
The well-stones teemed with ants, and children
Dropped coins to the top of his head. Pismire
Children. His mother came and said, Be patient.
I, she said, was always patient.
Faces came and went in the clear air overhead.
She was like everyone, expecting him to rape
The first wet thing he touched.

YMCA

At five you drive to town to chase off age.
You wait outside until the boys have left.
By then it's dark. Grown men with kids who'll starve
Without you unslam your pickups and slink
Inside. The young man in the chain-link cage
Accepts your wallet: *Nothing there to lift,*
His light hands say. Your eyes, like minnows, carve
Your fat into his image. Things you think
He knows. Beyond you his young eyes laugh
While you undress and vainly try to weave
Your legs with straps. Of course, your testes shrink.
Your buttocks wrinkle like an ancient face,
And the cloth lets sag the years no kiss can lift.
If there were more to spite, you too would laugh.

Travel Toward My Father's Funeral

1

East from San Francisco the silver train
Is choice, the silver rails are incorruptible.
Like clocks. Afterwards, gas lets dead men float.
Imagine that. Even death is full.
The Great Plains are repeating a green note.
Tirelessly. In this I have no say: green bone.
But the corpse is grey at the end of the trail.
Cold does it. Cold. The *it* that snows and rains
Without us. The engine pulls me one more breaststroke
Forward, beating blame into the crushed stone
They call a bed. Believe this: like a vast name
The distance leaves as if to stun
With distance. The horizon is too pale
For dawn, too dull to cut my father's throat.

2

I fall asleep between boxed lunch and baggage.
The dream is Hawaii passed, a ship in the night.
Atlas is easy: Pearl Harbor, Plymouth Rock,
Vladivostok, Mongolia, the Kirghiz Steppe.
I rise in the tingle of an obscene print.
I wake up with a hard-on and then, with luck,
Drift back into crossed worlds and camouflage.
I remember a fellow whose hand shapes
Someone's thigh. The dream recurs, fingers tight
On my leg. I panic at the wrong stop,
Maybe Hartford. He makes his move. Bridgeport
Is what I should have come to, had I slept.
Outside, Japan stirs. A rough edge scrapes
The Pacific. Japan is a rising clock.

3

Now, when I'm sure he's wide awake, we tour
The train from stem to stern and can decide:
The engine's pushing progress from the rear.
But the circle is uncertain. It won't allow
Our jumping from the finish to the start.
We're kissing our arse goodbye. The cowcatcher broods
Like little brother's last bucktooth.
Behind him, in cold air, parallel Kansases tire
Our eyes, so we turn and retrace the great truths.
Passing through the coal car you are mistaken for coal.
Helpful, sweaty firemen feed you into the hot heart.
Their hands are strong. What makes me run is fuel.
In a train as long as its circling track
This going forward has to mean we're going back.

4

In my last dream I find my father dead
Near a Russian village overrun
By children awaiting the outbreak of war.
Everyone would like to buy my gun.
I claim my father's body and buy two tickets
For the train that will carry us to Poland.
We meet Christ and the Inquisitor
Leaving the dining car. We talk. We peer
Through the frosted windows at the fast snow
Creating the countryside. I say: This land
Seems slower under snow. The *Sanctus* bells
Fill the next village or one we passed before.
Who says your son is sorry? death foretells
Decay? nowhere left to go? Who could know?

Cemetery Art

The Huns come through. They knock the parts off
Some handsome gods. The damages are stunning.
One looks down. Lost. The living proof like agates
In a marble game. Lost! The dark complaint,
Omoi! omoi! And now he is reduced to sunning
On Olympus's shady side with the faggots.
Then the draft. The doctor has him drop, please, cough
Into a thumb. This is the chiseler's cold steel tool.
The doctor is a sculptor in his dreary world:
Pull down thy cerements, pull down and cough.
It uses so much blood I always faint.
What the Huns have knocked apart stays wrecked.
He was not born like this, he thinks; he was hexed
By great art and the ways it registers complaint.

54

Teaching My Horses to Read

One dark eye always looked away like
January and the wind took care of pages.
They chose anything: death, love, hearts that leak
Chamber to chamber, geometry, the stages
The Horse went through. What they'd been missing
Was the world beyond pasture when gods lived
And men breathed water. They were kissing
The leaves of the book and, had I not loved
Strange unalterable air, I'd have said
They were mistaking the pages for food.
Behind them, always, some danger about to erupt.
Overnight, grass became jimson and the dead
Browsed until dawn. They left nothing good.
Nothing one learned cannot delight or corrupt.

A Note About the Author

Thomas Rabbitt was born in Boston, Massachusetts, in 1943
and was educated at the Boston Latin School and Harvard College.
He received his M.A. from Johns Hopkins University and
his M.F.A. from The University of Iowa. His first book of poems,
Exile, was the winner of the Pitt Prize (The U.S. Award
of the International Poetry Forum). He lives in Buhl, Alabama,
and teaches at the University of Alabama in Tuscaloosa.

A Note on the Type

The text of this book was set in a face called Cheltenham Old Style, designed by the architect Bertram Grosvenor Goodhue in collaboration with Ingalls Kimball of The Cheltenham Press of New York. Cheltenham was introduced in the early twentieth century, a period of remarkable achievement in type design. The idea of creating a "family" of types by making variations on the basic type design was originated by Goodhue and Kimball in the design of the Cheltenham series.

Composed by Superior Printing, Champaign, Illinois
Printed and bound by American Book-Stratford Press,
Saddle Brook, New Jersey

Typography and binding design by Dorothy Schmiderer

k

$5.95

Knopf Poetry Series, 3

The Booth Interstate is the second collection of poems by the celebrated young poet whose first book, *Exile*, won the U.S. Award of the International Poetry Forum in 1975.

This new book opens with a haunting and beautiful sonnet sequence about country life, country violence, and country peace—coon hunts, haybales, weevils, cotton flower, dogs and chickens, legends—and, above all, country people: a boy thinking how sometimes "The smell of a girl would stay in the wool / Like beer..."; a widow finding her son dead in a hollow in the heart of winter, "In January / Death lies down and grafts itself to roots"; the intensity of a vivid and eccentric country woman, "For fifty-seven years her hair is red / And her bright pinafores amaze the flowers"; a young girl drowning in a local pond, "Her broken heart / Drives down and darkly to the vegetating edge."

There are, as well, poems set in dreams, on Cape Cod, in Poland, in Russia, and meticulous, tender silhouettes—of a gargoyle, of a weathercock ("He knows the moon was cast / Of bronze and set adrift in clouds sour with rain"). And there is a passionate poem, *Views from the Bridge*, in homage to two poets who destroyed themselves—to Crane, and to Berryman, "I could let go / But for the strange man hanging to my neck / Who's still afraid."

These are poems that startle by their simplicity, craft, and feeling—in every way a fresh pleasure, and a singular achievement.

Alfred A. Knopf, Publisher, New York

Cover sculpture by David Smith

Cover design by Janet Odgis

3/81

394-73962-0